FROM STRESS TO
SUCCESS...
in Just 31 Days!

Also by Dr. John F. Demartini

The Breakthrough Experience: *A Revolutionary New Approach to Personal Transformation*

Count Your Blessings: *The Healing Power of Gratitude and Love*

The Heart of Love: *How to Go Beyond Fantasy to Find True Relationship Fulfillment*

How to Make One Hell of a Profit and Still Get to Heaven

The Riches Within: *Your Seven Secret Treasures*

You Can Have an Amazing Life . . . in Just 60 Days!

All of the above are available at your
local bookstore, or may be ordered by visiting:

Hay House USA: **www.hayhouse.com**®
Hay House Australia: **www.hayhouse.com.au**
Hay House UK: **www.hayhouse.co.uk**
Hay House South Africa: **www.hayhouse.co.za**
Hay House India: **www.hayhouse.co.in**

FROM STRESS TO
SUCCESS...
in Just 31 Days!

Dr. John F. Demartini

HAY HOUSE, INC.
Carlsbad, California • New York City
London • Sydney • Johannesburg
Vancouver • Hong Kong • New Delhi

Published and distributed in the United States by: Hay House, Inc.: www
.hayhouse.com • *Published and distributed in Australia by:* Hay House
Australia Pty. Ltd.: www.hayhouse.com.au • *Published and distributed in the
United Kingdom by:* Hay House UK, Ltd.: www.hayhouse.co.uk • *Published
and distributed in the Republic of South Africa by:* Hay House SA (Pty),
Ltd.: www.hayhouse.co.za • *Distributed in Canada by:* Raincoast: www
.raincoast.com • *Published in India by:* Hay House Publishers India: www
.hayhouse.co.in

Editorial supervision: Jill Kramer • *Design:* Jen Kennedy

Library of Congress Cataloging-in-Publication Data

Demartini, John F.
  From stress to success-- in just 31 days / John F. Demartini. -- 1st ed.
    p. cm.
  ISBN 978-1-4019-2299-3 (hardcover : alk. paper) 1. Success. 2. Stress
management. I. Title.
  BF637.S8D369 2009
  158.1--dc22

                                    2008032978

ISBN: 978-1-4019-2299-3

12 11 10 09   4 3 2 1
1st edition, July 2009

Printed in the United States of America

*From Stress to Success . . .
in Just 31 Days!* is dedicated to
those individuals who are truly ready to
apply powerful and practical action steps to
their daily routines, which will help them transform
their perceived stresses into achieved successes.
It is for those who are certain they are ready
to live more fulfilling and inspired lives!

Contents

Introduction

Most people don't mind stress as long as it's someone else's and they don't have to deal with it. Of course you know that stress impacts your life—everyone knows that. But what if you could turn that stress into success? What kind of life could you then lead?

Could you save energy instead of spending it? Could you direct your life instead of being a slave to it? Could you build self-worth instead of destroying it? Could you love your relationships instead of sabotaging them?

Could you heal your body instead of disordering it? And could you sleep peacefully instead of tossing and turning every night? Could you simply *live a greater life?*

Of course you can!

No matter who you are or what you do, stress impacts success in each of the seven areas of life: spiritual, mental, vocational, financial, familial, social, and physical.

Moreover, success means many things to many people. For instance, everyone would love to perform as well as possible in their careers. Nobody enjoys being a failure, and successful individuals help those around them succeed as well.

We'd all love to have enough money to explore whatever our dreams and visions guide us to do. And it's certainly stressful when we're unable to do something or are limited in what we can experience due to a shortage of finances.

In addition, family and personal-relationship interactions can make or break the feeling of fulfillment in other areas. For example, it isn't much fun going home each night to a partner who's unappreciative of you, despite the fact that your colleagues think you're exceptional.

Also, becoming popular and well respected within a social network is a key part of feeling and being a success. A person without a circle of friends and associates is like someone who's stranded on an island without food or water . . . and that's certainly stressful.

On top of that, if you're ill or tired all the time and don't enjoy great health and energy, it can override any other successes because you always feel as if you're behind the eight ball. And this mind-set definitely doesn't breed success.

Our spiritual outlook and the values we strive for must be fulfilled for us to feel truly successful. Without spiritual fulfillment, how can there be genuine success?

And, of course, if we don't think that we're using our fullest mental capacities and expressing our unique talents and genius, we certainly won't believe that we've attained success. This can add even more stress to our lives.

Although the word *success* takes many forms and can mean various things, in this book, it will be more inclusive than exclusive and will signify overall fulfillment. Would you love to experience more success in each of the seven areas of your life? Do you wish to feel less stress? Then keep reading. . . .

The first step to achieving a more successful and fulfilling life is to alleviate stress, and this book is designed to do just that. Wouldn't it be wonderful to be able to just follow simple daily steps that will reduce stress and produce more success? Well, you can!

The following list comprises the 31 secrets that are your steps to success. You may be wondering, *Why are they called "secrets"?*

Well, even though some people have heard many of these statements before, few seem to take them to heart or live by them. Their wisdom is simple yet profound, and they're the secrets of the individuals who live more self-actualized lives.

Those who don't follow these simple steps often live their lives at the whims of others, each day experiencing quiet desperation and reaction. But those who implement these secrets daily enjoy empowering inspiration. The former endure lives of stress filled with strangling weeds, and the latter savor lives of success overflowing with blooming flowers. Which type of life would you rather lead?

Let's take a look at the daily stress-to-success secrets:

Stress-to-Success Secrets

On a daily basis:

1. Write and read your goals.
2. Clear away your goal's obstacles.
3. Prioritize your activities.
4. Act on top priorities.
5. Visualize your success.
6. Write and read your affirmations.
7. Practice deep breathing and stretching.

8. Do selective and collective reading.
9. Groom for success.
10. Dress for success.
11. Love what you do and do what you love.
12. Surround yourself with succeeders.
13. Drink lots of water.
14. Eat light, moderate meals.
15. Reduce the four "addictors."
16. Contract and then relax all muscles.
17. Help others fulfill their goals.
18. Save 5 to 10 percent of your earnings.
19. Write three thank-you letters.
20. Reward yourself for your accomplishments.
21. Express feelings of love.
22. Hug someone special.
23. Clean and organize your environment.
24. Eliminate low-priority "unnecessities."
25. Study the subject you'd love to master.
26. Spend time in total meditative silence.
27. Massage your body or scalp.
28. Take a hot bath before retiring.
29. Count your blessings with gratitude.
30. Get a good night's rest.
31. Follow a Stress-to-Success Checklist.

Carefully study these secrets. Incorporating them into your life will reveal the magic inherent in each step and help you transform your stress into success.

Now let's examine each of the daily success secrets step-by-step and expand upon them.

Secret #1

WRITE AND READ YOUR GOALS

Each of us, way deep inside, has goals involving the seven areas of life. Some of these may be long-term or even lifetime ones, and other dreams or desires are simply for more immediate gratification.

Just as you experience great bursts of quick kinetic energy when you're striving to accomplish short-term objectives, there's also enormous potential power in having long-term and lifetime goals. Both types are valuable and serve each other. In order to be successful in achieving a short- or long-term desire or goal, you must place your focus on the end result and apply discipline on either a moment-to-moment, day-to-day, month-to-month, or year-to-year level.

For example, if a farmer is to plow a straight furrow, he must keep his eye on a distant point or on the horizon. If his focus is directed just a few feet ahead of his tractor, his plowing will waver. Even though the wheels of his tractor move over short turns and distances, in order for his field to be plowed straight, he must know *and* focus on his long-term vision and aim.

Focusing on a long-term goal or desire can provide the enthusiasm and energy to get things done in the present. For instance, when a runner sets a goal to run a mile, she'll probably be tired when she reaches the one-mile mark. But if this same runner sets a goal to run ten miles, she probably won't even be sweating upon passing this same one-mile mark. If this very same, determined runner were to set a goal to run 26 miles and keep her mind on the completion of this marathon, not only wouldn't she be sweating, but most likely she wouldn't even be winded as she whisked by the one-mile mark.

Long-term goals, however, can't be accomplished without first succeeding in intermediate short-term goals. We may have a goal to climb a ladder, but we have to put a foot on each rung in order to reach the top.

PRACTICAL ACTION STEPS

1. Each morning before you rise from your bed, meditate on your innermost dreams or goals.

2. Ask for guidance from the highest and most inspired part of yourself.

3. Keep a notepad next to your bed and write down whatever goals become revealed. If no specific lifetime goal is revealed but short-term ones are, that's great! At least you've made a step on your ladder—and like the game of *Concentration*, the short-term goals will eventually reveal a solution to the puzzle.

4. Write and read these goals daily.

AFFIRMATIONS

My goals are clear. They are written from my heart. I can see my light upon the horizon.

Now write your own affirmation in your journal
or on a separate piece of paper.

Secret #2

CLEAR AWAY YOUR GOAL'S OBSTACLES

Sometimes it's hard to imagine yourself achieving a goal, particularly if it's of some magnitude. In your imagination, such a goal can become clouded by obstacles, but limiting your dreams simply because they seem too difficult to reach is unwise. Instead, it's much more beneficial to clear away the obstacles by breaking your goal down into smaller actions. Let's look at accomplishing something that appears difficult, or even impossible, at first thought.

Imagine that someone bet you a million dollars that you couldn't eat an *entire elephant.* If you thought about eating the elephant in one sitting, you'd immediately become grossly overwhelmed by the very notion.

But if there wasn't a time frame on the bet, and you planned to eat that elephant one small bite at a time, the possibility of achieving your goal and winning the million-dollar bet isn't so wildly far-fetched after all.

If you let them, your many stressful obstacles will seem to mount up just like elephants at times. They'll be the giant mountains that you have to figure out how to climb and conquer.

If you were to look at all your obstacles as a whole, you might become defeated and filled with fear (and thereby stressed). But if you break these big obstacles down into smaller, more manageable bites, you can consume these daily elephants with ease.

Transform your elephants of stress into small bites of delight! Should you encounter an overwhelming action step in any day, change its corresponding stress into success by chunking it down further into smaller substeps. It's true that *any action taken by the yard can be hard, yet by the inch, it suddenly becomes a cinch.*

Stop creating stress by attempting to accomplish elephant-sized actions immediately. Instead, foster ease and success by chunking obstacles down into small pieces that you can tackle.

For example, I can recall a time when the magic of "chunking" was required to overcome one of my obstacles. I once made a commitment to myself to write a book, and I imagined it to be about 200 pages in length. At first, the thought of this project seemed totally overwhelming and a major obstacle. I found myself procrastinating. Weeks went by before I finally remembered the value of breaking down large projects into bite-sized action steps. I then chunked my book down into daily actions steps and committed myself to writing just five pages a day. In six weeks, the book was completed!

Once I chunked the book down, the pressure and stress were off, and the words seemed to flow out of me. Today, this book is still selling around the world.

PRACTICAL ACTION STEPS

1. Write down one of your goals that you'd love to accomplish but feel overwhelmed by.

2. Next, list seven or fewer of the highest priority action steps that you could do that would allow you to accomplish this goal.

3. If any one of these smaller action steps still feels overwhelming, chunk each one down even further into smaller actions. Keep chunking your actions until you feel that you have a clear road ahead to the accomplishment of your goal.

4. After you've chunked this overwhelming and stressful goal down into easy action-step bites, then decide the priority that you would love to do them in.

AFFIRMATION

I accomplish my big goals one simple step at a time.

Now write your own affirmation in your journal or on a separate piece of paper.

Secret #3

PRIORITIZE YOUR ACTIVITIES

To prioritize is to organize, and to organize is to transform stress into success. Thus, you're rewarded in life to the degree that you can master the ability to organize stressful disorder.

Successful people plan and prioritize their lives: they focus on ABC issues. Stressful people live an unplanned, unorganized life and work on XYZ issues.

To fail to plan is to plan to fail. Determining what's truly most important in your life and in your daily actions is one of the wisest things you can do.

You'll find that those who live their lives without prioritizing feel as if they run out of time each day, accomplishing practically nothing. They get lost along their life's path and usually end up draining other people's energy because they need to be rescued. However, those who do prioritize tend to have more spare time at the end of the day and feel that they're high achievers. In fact, those who plan get ahead and stay ahead of daily disorder.

High-priority actions are like flowers. If you don't focus on them and cultivate and nurture them, your garden of life becomes entangled in low-priority weeds.

Don't confuse busyness with productivity. You may have had a day filled with "things to do," but they may have just been fires to put out. Low-priority "fires" and random "things" won't make you feel or become successful. In fact, they just add to your stress level. If you don't fill your day with high-priority actions, somehow it becomes overrun by low-priority fires and stresses.

In all probability, no one else will prioritize your daily actions—it's up to you. Successful people determine what's truly important in their lives and make those things a top priority.

PRACTICAL ACTION STEPS

1. Each morning, before starting your day, decide what the seven highest priority action steps are that you can do that day to help you bring more fulfilling success into your life.

2. Write down those seven action steps and carry them with you throughout the day. Do this every day.

3. Think about and then jot down today's seven highest priority action steps right now.

AFFIRMATION

I plan my day, I prioritize my plan, and I am productive because of this priority.

Now write your own affirmation in your journal or on a separate piece of paper.

11

Secret #4

ACT ON TOP PRIORITIES

It was Mary Kay Ash of Mary Kay cosmetics who built an international company by simply asking herself every day: *What are the highest priority action steps I can do today that will help me fulfill my life's work?* She simply wrote them down daily—and most important, she developed the habit and discipline of following through on them.

Just as you learned to develop the habit and discipline of brushing your teeth, you can also learn to develop the habit and discipline of *acting on top priorities*. You probably have a routine that you follow when brushing your teeth either upon arising or after eating. It's just as wise to determine and then maintain a routine when building the discipline to be focused on top-priority actions throughout your day. In some cases, hourly checks on yourself can prove helpful.

PRACTICAL ACTION STEPS

1. Make a habit out of acting on your seven highest priority action steps. Writing them down each morning is the first step. Now is the time to create a daily routine and cultivate success.

2. To keep yourself on track, put your written list in front of you or in a place where it's easily seen so that it's constantly reminding you of your priorities throughout the day. If you're at home, you may place this list on a mirror, by the phone, or on a table. You could also keep it in your pocket or wallet, or simply pin the list to your sleeve. If you're at the office, you may wish to put it right in front of you on your desk. The more obvious your list is to you, the more likely you are to follow your prioritized action steps.

3. Ask a friend or loved one to help you until you've established the discipline of this new habit—that is, until it's second nature to you. (For example, when you were a child, you may have needed to be reminded to brush your teeth each day. Even though you're now an adult, it's still okay—and even beneficial—to ask for reminders from time to time to help you stay on task and be your best.)

AFFIRMATION

I am disciplined, and I focus on my top priorities; therefore, I am successful.

Now write your own affirmation in your journal or on a separate piece of paper.

Secret #5

VISUALIZE YOUR SUCCESS

It was Bill Cosby who once said, "What you sees is what you gets [*sic*]." This statement says a lot in that our lives follow our visions. A lack of, or unclear, vision creates stress, but focused vision leads to order and success. This is the reason why details are so important.

If our vision lacks focus, we must write down more details in our action steps. Our vitality in life is directly proportionate to the vividness of our vision of success. In fact, fatigue, depression, and stress are often simply due to a lack of clarity. If we can't see our success, or what we need to do in order to create it, how can we expect to live it?

For example, pro golfers, basketball players, and architects all must envision their success clearly in their minds before they can achieve their success in real life. Our marvelous brains and bodies tend to work most efficiently when they have a distinct, planned picture to work on. To visualize is to create an inner blueprint for success.

Your body and life's direction follow your inner visions; and if you create a clear, detailed blueprint, it will be easy to carry out. Those with the clearest vision tend to lead those whose vision is cloudy. In addition, they experience more success and less stress, which is why others look to them for guidance. To lead a successful life means to visualize one clearly.

PRACTICAL ACTION STEPS

1. After writing and reading your prioritized action steps, take at least five minutes to visualize a stress-free and simple completion of each one.

2. Focus on the details! The more specific you are, the easier it is to follow through on your action steps.

3. Most important, visualize the outcome as well as the journey. See yourself successfully achieving each of these steps until you feel the satisfaction of their completion. Enjoy this feeling. The mind initially creates a virtual reality that eventually manifests into reality. (Remember that successful professionals practice in between performances. They regularly perceive themselves accomplishing tasks and attaining success with their mind's eye.)

AFFIRMATION

I can see myself succeeding; it is done.
Wow, what a feeling!

Now write your own affirmation in your journal
or on a separate piece of paper.

19

Secret #6

WRITE AND READ YOUR AFFIRMATIONS

Our lives are reflections of our self-talk. What we constantly say to ourselves is what becomes our reality. For example, if we constantly tell ourselves, or even others, that we're stupid, we tend to follow up with stupid actions because that's what we expect from ourselves.

If you keep saying that you're forgetful, you're talking yourself into forgetting. If you tell yourself that you're wise and healthy, you'll tend toward that as your reality. Your words are creative by nature.

As an example of how self-talk can create reality, let's look at my story:

When I was 17, I met a famous doctor named Paul Bragg who gave me one of the most profound gifts of my life: an affirmation that was filled with words of power. To this very day, I still say it: *I am a genius, and I apply my wisdom.*

At the time, I was a high-school dropout and was living in a tent in Hawaii. I had a very limited vocabulary and had never finished reading a single book. When Dr. Bragg taught me this affirmation, he told me to say it with feeling as if it were true and present. To do so seemed so far from reality that it was funny. However, after stumbling many times in saying it, I finally began to feel what those powerful words meant. So every day I continued to say it, and it became easier to believe: *I am a genius, and I apply my wisdom.*

It was two and a half years later when I really saw the results of the affirmation. I was sitting in a college library surrounded by fellow students I was tutoring in calculus. I heard one of the students whisper to another, "That John, he's a f---ing genius!" At that moment, I remembered what Dr. Bragg had taught me, and I made a commitment to say this statement, and many others like it, for the rest of my life.

I can't sufficiently put into words what a difference this affirmation and the many others like it have made in my life. Because of them, I was able to transform from a high-school dropout to the top of my classes all the way through professional school. I believe that the key to affirmations is putting your heartfelt feelings into them and saying them over and over every day.

PRACTICAL ACTION STEPS

1. To move from stress to success, transpose your list of goals and high-priority action steps into affirmation statements. If your dream is to become a multimillionaire, then specifically state it as such. For example: *I am a multimillionaire who is constantly aware of moneymaking opportunities.*

2. Each day, reread and rewrite (for extra effect) your highest priority affirmations.

3. Say your affirmations with feeling, and as if they were already true.

AFFIRMATION

*My affirmations are true, and I say them
from my heart every day.*

Now write your own affirmation in your journal
or on a separate piece of paper.

Secret #7

PRACTICE DEEP BREATHING
AND STRETCHING

If we listen to our bodies—through their aches or pains, as well as their cycles of sleep, activity, or tiredness—they tell us lots of information about ourselves, our lives, and our physical conditions. Our bodies are constantly guiding us to success. When we listen, success is ours; when we don't, our lives become filled with stress.

When you're feeling stressed, you generally have difficulty breathing and experience tightness throughout your body. When you feel "successed," you experience ease of breath and looseness throughout your body. Stress is constriction—while success is expansion and freedom.

To transform stress into success, we must develop the skill of listening and relaxing. To become successful, we often must act as if we're already successful. Success breeds success just as failure breeds failure. One way in which we can relax and succeed is by gaining control over our diaphragm and other muscles.

Can you recall a time when you felt stressed and automatically took a deep breath and stretched in order to feel more at ease? Somehow you intuitively knew that breathing and stretching would provide some relief. Why wait until you're stressed and fall behind? Why not develop the habit of relaxation and success to get ahead?

PRACTICAL ACTION STEPS

For the next five minutes, do the following stretches while breathing through your nose. If you're comfortable doing so, they're best done while standing. But if this isn't possible, you can alter them or replace them with breathing or other exercises that you can perform. It's important that you don't strain or force yourself. These are merely for relaxation and integration.

1. While standing and breathing out, gently and carefully bend forward and downward at the waist, reaching your hands toward the floor. Then inhale, and slowly bend upward and backward, putting your hands up toward the ceiling behind you. Repeat this five times.

2. While standing and exhaling, gently and carefully bend to the right and downward at the waist, and bring your right hand toward the floor. Then upon breathing inward, slowly straighten up. Reverse this same procedure, and do it from your left side. Repeat this five times on each side.

3. While standing and breathing out, gently and carefully twist to the right at the waist, bringing your shoulders at right angles to your feet. Upon breathing in, return to the forward position. Reverse this same procedure for the left side. Repeat five times on each side.

4. While standing, roll your neck around on your shoulders—gently! As your neck and head go back, breathe in. As your neck and head go forward, breathe out. Repeat five times.

5. While sitting in a comfortable upright position, slowly take a deep, deep breath to the count of five. Then hold this breath in to the count of three. Slowly and completely breathe out to the count of five. Hold this to the count of three, and then begin the breathing cycle all over again. Repeat this five times.

AFFIRMATION

I am stretching beyond my limitations and breathing inspiration into my actions.

Now write your own affirmation in your journal or on a separate piece of paper.

ಶಂ ಶಂ ಶಂ

Secret #8

DO SELECTIVE AND COLLECTIVE READING

There's an old saying that is wise to remember: "You cannot put your hand into a pot of glue without some of the glue sticking." So, too, you can't immerse your mind into the thoughts of others without some of their ideas "sticking" with you. If you expose your mind to the gloomy, doomy stresses of others, their anxieties may stick with you. If, in the morning, you read in the newspaper about how stressful people's lives are, you can attune to and become stuck in that same level of stress.

Be selective in what you read. Out of all of the possible reading materials you have available, choose those that will focus you on success the most. Collect inspirational, motivational stories from newspapers, magazines, or books.

29

If you don't focus on and put your hand into stories of success, you'll probably find yourself surrounded by the entangling stresses of the rest. There are numerous biographies of successful individuals available, as well as inspiring books of poetry and books of motivating and energizing quotations.

There's another saying that says, "People read books to remind them that they are not alone." So if you're naturally selective about the company you keep, why not be equally selective about the kind of authors or books you read?

PRACTICAL ACTION STEPS

1. Next to your bathroom commode, keep a book of inspirational short stories or poems. Read at least one page every time you're there to sit.

2. On your breakfast table, keep another book of inspirational or motivational stories or quotes. Read a page every time you sit there.

3. At both your home workstation and on your office desk, set down another book of inspirational biographies, short stories, or quotes. Read a page every time you're there and in need of a relaxing break.

4. If you read the newspaper, see how many upbeat or success stories you can collect and compile. These can be great conversation pieces to share, possibly throughout the day.

AFFIRMATIONS

I focus on the successful, motivating stories of others. I am inspired to greatness!

Now write your own affirmation in your journal or on a separate piece of paper.

Secret #9

GROOM FOR SUCCESS

Have you ever been out in public when you looked your worst? If you're like most people, you have, and you may recall this experience as one of your most embarrassing moments! If you ran into someone you knew or who knew you, you probably didn't feel your best or most confident . . . now did you?

The way we look does have an impact on our stress level. Even though we'd like to think that other people's opinions don't mean all that much, in most cases, they mean a lot more than we're willing to admit.

Bad-hair days, dirty nails, chipped nail polish, not-so-fresh breath, or times when you've gone out after just throwing something on certainly don't add to your success. You simply don't feel your best when you don't groom for success.

Why throw away easy confidence by not taking a few extra moments to groom and shine? You aren't just doing this for the reactions of others, but because of the reactions within yourself. Self-care fosters self-worth, and you never know what opportunities might be waiting for you each day.

It pays for you to engage in a personal grooming routine so that you feel great at all times. By doing so, you can't help but have more confidence and even more love for yourself. Looking your best helps transform stress into success.

PRACTICAL ACTION STEPS

Every morning . . .

1. Take a bath or shower.

2. Check your nails for length, cleanliness, and/or polish.

3. Brush and floss your teeth—use mouth-wash, too.

4. Comb, brush, and style your hair.

5. Trim any straggling, stray hairs and/or shave as needed.

6. Wear a bit of cologne or perfume.

7. Apply some makeup.

8. [Jot down another practical action step that will help you groom for success.]

AFFIRMATIONS

Thank you, my body.
I love you, and I groom you well.

Now write your own affirmation in your journal or on a separate piece of paper.

৵৹ ৵৹ ৵৹

Secret #10

DRESS FOR SUCCESS

Can the way you dress impact how people respond to or treat you? Could a person's first impression of you partly determine the outcome of your daily activities or dealings? Can what you wear make you feel more or less confident? Can dressing for success help you bring about success? The answer is *yes* to all these questions!

Most of us have felt the impact that clothes have on us. After all, the entire fashion industry has been built and maintained by the power that has been attached to clothing. Cultures all over the world recognize social status in relationship to clothing hierarchies. Each of the brand names, labels, and styles have their buyers— some for the more common and others for the elite.

As an example of the effects of our clothing choices, I'd like to share a couple of firsthand experiences:

I once walked into a men's fine apparel store dressed in a jogging outfit and sneakers. After looking at a row of moderate to high-end Armani suits for a few moments, a salesman finally approached me.

As he motioned to another area of the store, his first words to me were: "I think what you're looking for, sir, would be over in this section. I think these suits will fit into your price range."

My mouth just dropped when he said that to me. I couldn't believe that he'd sized me up in this way, and I felt that he'd judged my book by its cover! I left the store soon thereafter while realizing that if I ever returned, I would dress better than I had.

On another occasion, I was at a grocery store standing in line at a checkout counter. I was wearing running shorts and a sweaty T-shirt. I suddenly noticed one of my patients standing three people ahead of me in line. She was talking with another woman who, I later discovered, was her friend.

As I walked up to her and exchanged pleasantries, I noticed her eyes scanning me up and down as if surprised and embarrassed. She didn't introduce me to her friend, nor did she say anything to me that might give away to this other person that I was her doctor. There was simply an unspoken uneasiness.

Although our lives aren't meant to be totally run by other people's reactions, their reactions are often reflections of our own. They just help us become aware that we aren't taking the time to reflect our most empowered selves. When we don't spend that extra moment to dress for success, many of us are caught off guard by others' (and, ultimately, our own) reactions. This is a lesson that helps us confirm that what we wear *does* make a difference. We can actually dress in such a way that adds to our stress and hinders success, or we can choose to build our success and reduce stress. It's that simple.

You also don't necessarily have to spend outrageous sums of money to dress nicely. A lot of great clothing can be purchased and coordinated at a moderate cost.

In addition, well-planned timing and patience (such as waiting to buy items during sales) can save you many dollars. Oftentimes, owning fewer, but higher quality, outfits is better than having a lot of random pieces of clothing. And enduring classics are commonly wiser investments than trendy fads.

PRACTICAL ACTION STEPS

1. Clean out your closet and drawers of all the clothes and shoes that make you feel just so-so or drab when you put them on. If you don't feel your best when you wear them, why hold on to them? Maybe they'll look great on someone else. Give them away!

2. Organize the remaining clothes you have into as many fabulous outfit combinations as you can. Clean and press them, if needed.

3. Each day, wear whatever outfit makes you feel your best—most confident, most alert, most sharp, most clever . . . your most successful self.

AFFIRMATION

Every day, I dress for success and look my best.

Now write your own affirmation in your journal
or on a separate piece of paper.

LOVE WHAT YOU DO AND
DO WHAT YOU LOVE

It's so easy to meander off the most direct highway to success in life, which is the road that leads straight to the fulfillment of our goals and desires. When we detour from this pathway that our inner knowing, intuition, or inspiration has been guiding us toward, we diminish our success and create stress. But why don't we follow through on these inspired or intuitive ideas?

The primary reason is because we haven't learned to trust our own inner promptings; instead, we rely on our partners, friends, or advisers. The opinions of these well-intentioned people take precedence over our own wisdom, especially during times when we feel uncertain and filled with self-doubt, fear, or guilt. These stressful feelings stop us from doing what we would love to do, and we pay dearly for not following our hearts. In fact, we feel disrupted and surely not our best. This is called stress! So often we do things out of fear or desperation instead of inspiration.

It's much wiser not to act from a despondent state of mind. To trust and follow inspiration is wisdom of the highest, brightest kind. Our self-worth is enhanced when we act on what we love, and it's hindered when we don't. When our heart is into what we do, the work is done more successfully. But when we act out of desperation, we just create more stress.

You don't have to create stress or act out of desperation. Even if you're in a career that isn't fulfilling, you don't have to perceive yourself as being trapped or in a hopeless situation. If you simply immerse yourself wholeheartedly into your vocation, you can and will attract greater opportunities that will then allow you to do more of what you love.

Loving what you do leads to doing what you love. Whatever you're presently doing would be wisely perceived as being a stepping-stone to ever-greater "doings" ahead. But if you aren't ready to just step out there and start doing what you love immediately, at least put your heart into what you're doing now. While engaged in this, begin your planning and preparing for creating what you love tomorrow.

Oftentimes, when you put your heart into what you're doing, you discover that it's truly what you love after all. When you do what you love and love what you do, you transform work into play and stress into success.

PRACTICAL ACTION STEPS

1. If you feel that you aren't doing what you love, write down at least 20 benefits of whatever you are currently doing. As you're writing this list, keep in mind that whatever you're engaged in is simply a stepping-stone. It's preparing you for what you would love to do tomorrow. This will help you put your heart more fully into your day.

2. If you do feel that you're already doing what
    you love, write down a long list of its ben-
    efits. Keep writing until you feel your heart
    open up even more to your daily life.

AFFIRMATION

I do what I love, and I love what I do.

Now write your own affirmation in your journal
or on a separate piece of paper.

෧෨ඁ ෧෨ඁ ෧෨ඁ

Secret #12

SURROUND YOURSELF
WITH SUCCEEDERS

Do birds of a feather flock together? It certainly appears that they do. We tend to hang around with individuals who are similar to ourselves. Poor people tend to surround themselves with other poor people, and rich people with other rich people. Intelligent people associate with like minds, and artists typically seek out other artists.

It appears that we all have comfort zones we attempt to stay within. Very stressed and impoverished people don't feel comfortable associating with more self-actualized and enriched people.

We owe it to each other to be successful because success breeds more success. And if we aren't feeling successful, looking at who we have as friends and associates can tell us and others a lot about ourselves and why. The longer we associate with a group of individuals, the more our thinking and feeling processes become like theirs, or vice versa.

A few years ago, a doctor friend of mine began associating with a new group of people. At the time, he had a successful practice and a broad and apparently grateful outlook on life. However, within the first six months of his association with these individuals, his attitude and goals shifted significantly. He was angry at how things were and was constantly blaming those who'd become his opposition. He was more issue oriented and very opinionated. As a result, his practice dropped in quality of service. His facial expressions often showed anger and tension.

After about two years of association with this group, he learned some valuable lessons. He realized that constantly focusing on problems or blaming others doesn't lead to a rewarding life, nor does it solve as much as it ends up creating new problems and issues. He decided that he'd rather get back into serving his patients.

This doctor put his heart and attention on his practice, and his life changed. He began to attract people who focused on life-expanding ideas and solutions instead of problems. His success was now more apparent than his stress—his fulfillment more apparent than his frustration.

Whom we hang out with *does* make a difference. The old saying "If you want to soar with the eagles, don't flock with the turkeys" has merit.

In society, people are power, and our social network often correlates to our outlook. More successful and fulfilled people tend to associate with other successful and fulfilled people. Stressed-out individuals often join with like minds who also wallow in their pity parties, trauma dramas, and ho-hum doldrums. It's the successful people who join with those who follow their dreams and make them come true.

PRACTICAL ACTION STEPS

1. Create an ongoing list starting with 20 people you know who are successful and

fulfilled in their lives, those who are doing what they love and loving what they do, and those who aren't just living but are truly loving life.

2. Read this list daily.

3. Contact and meet these people. Oftentimes, they're simply a telephone call away. Find out how they think, what they feel, how they view life, what they talk about, and whom they associate with. Ask them about their life philosophy. Tell them your goals, and ask them for leads to others who might help you become more fulfilled.

4. Surround yourself with people who are inspired by life; and watch before your very eyes how your own thoughts, actions, and life will change from stress to success.

AFFIRMATION

*I associate with success, and I surround
myself with inspired life builders.*

Now write your own affirmation in your journal
or on a separate piece of paper.

಄ ಄ ಄

Secret #13

DRINK LOTS OF WATER

Water has been called the universal solvent for millennia. It makes up between 80 and 90 percent of our bodies. Besides oxygen, it's the most important substance required for life. We may go without food for weeks, but our bodies demand water almost daily. Without it to flush our system, we become toxic; without it to expand our cells and maintain our physical chemistry, we die. Water is truly a gift of life—no cell can live without it.

But marketing gurus have successfully convinced the public that soft drinks, fruit juices, and other beverages that can make them hoards of money are what our bodies truly crave and enjoy. It's amazing how many people don't consume enough pure water.

There's something special about plain water—not just liquids, but good old H_2O. Some of the signs of not drinking enough of it are crankiness, irritability, and fatigue, as well as stiffness, mental cloudiness, and sometimes other health disorders, including constipation, dry eyes, dry skin, difficulty breathing, headaches, stiff joints, and more.

I've seen many people make major shifts in their outlook on life once they simply began drinking more water. It increases our energy and helps us maintain a brighter, clearer view of life.

Many people notice that their various health problems clear up once they increase their water intake. Whether it be distilled, spring, deionized, or even mineral water is less important than the idea of it being consumed. We're a nation of cleaner *outer* bodies than *inner* ones. Water is the great cleanser of our bodies, minds, and spirits.

It's been said that "vitality is power minus obstruction." Here, the "obstructions" are washed away with water. It cleans out our circulatory systems and helps regulate our blood-sugar levels. When we consume it wisely, water can change our lives of stress into lives of success.

PRACTICAL ACTION STEPS

1. Upon waking, drink a glass of water.

2. Throughout the day, keep a glass filled with water nearby to remind you to drink often.

3. Instead of drinking tea, coffee, alcohol, soft drinks, or even fruit juice, substitute it with water.

4. Simply develop a greater taste for water.

AFFIRMATIONS

I am clean, clear, and refreshed.
I sparkle as I drink my life-giving water.

Now write your own affirmation in your journal or on a separate piece of paper.

⌘ ⌘ ⌘

Secret #14

EAT LIGHT, MODERATE MEALS

There's great wisdom in the expression "You are what you eat." But there's an extra ingredient that needs to be added to this statement: not only is it "what you eat," but also *when* and *how much* you eat that tends to make you *you!*

Most of us have overeaten late at night and have felt "the blahs" the next day. Heavy late-night eating doesn't energize us or make us feel our best. In fact, it adds to our stress level. Besides consuming too much or too late at night, having no eating rhythm can also throw our bodies into a spin. Moderation, rhythm, and consistency are guiding principles when it comes to a healthy diet.

If you want to maximize your energy and build a life of success, it's wise to eat light in the evening and moderately during the day. Just as you know that it's a good idea to push away from the table before you're full, it's also best not to go straight to bed after a large meal. You'd feel much better if you walked off that stuffed-stomach sensation first. In addition, pigging out during the time when your circadian rhythm isn't metabolizing at its peak makes you sluggish.

Success demands energy. Eating heavy to gain more energy is like fighting for peace—it's contradictory. Moderation is the secret in normalizing extremes in mood, energy, and productivity. Eating earlier in the evening also helps you sleep better.

In addition to eating moderately and early in the day, be selective in what you eat. Before you put anything into your mouth, consider whether or not it's serving your success. Instead of being a robot to past habits (for example, eating just for the sake of eating or mindlessly eating until you're stuffed), consider the consequences. By eating only when you're truly hungry, eating less rather than more, and eating light at night, your whole body will feel more energized and in tune with success in life.

PRACTICAL ACTION STEPS

1. When you eat in the evening, prepare moderate-sized meals, preferably at least three hours before retiring. If you feel that you've eaten too much, don't lie down immediately; instead, go for a walk or do some gentle exercises to stimulate your metabolism. The lighter you eat, the sooner you can relax on the couch or go to bed.

2. Don't pig out! If you do find yourself over-eating, chew your food more times and eat more slowly. If you're dining out, simply don't order so much. When you're preparing meals at home, take out of the refrigerator or off the stove only the light, right proportion of food. Put the rest away so that you're not tempted to finish it off. This isn't the time to worry about starving children in China! It *is* the time to eat wisely so you can build tomorrow's success.

AFFIRMATIONS

I eat wisely.
Every bite I take builds my dreams of success.

Now write your own affirmation in your journal
or on a separate piece of paper.

෴ ෴ ෴

Secret #15

REDUCE THE FOUR "ADDICTORS"

We hear so much about the evils of addiction, but the goal of this book isn't to dwell on this topic. To expect everyone to completely eliminate their intake of the four "addictors"—coffee, cigarettes, alcohol, and sugar—would be too idealistic.

It would be more realistic, however, to emphasize the value of moderation. Extremes tend to breed their opposite, but moderation breeds success. That's the aim of this book!

Instead of making yourself feel bad about your addictions—which most people have in one form or another, anyway—master them by striving for moderation. Your body simply doesn't need these "addictors." In fact, you may be using them to relieve symptoms that are a result of not following the other stress-to-success suggestions. For example, if you feel sluggish in the mornings, you may turn to coffee to provide a temporary buzz, but if it's used in excess, it can disturb the energy-producing processes of the liver and pancreas. That certainly won't help your success.

Smoking cigarettes, particularly if you're a chain-smoker, can rob your lungs of oxygen and shrink your blood vessels so that your cells can't survive. Since life and success go together, this would be wise to moderate.

Alcohol in moderation may not be unwise but certainly in excess can be your demise. To sip and not guzzle is smart. Drinking for the sake of drinking is probably not the highest priority action step on the path to success. Although alcohol may appear to provide a temporary high, what goes up must come down. So control it, before it controls you.

In the same way that your brain needs oxygen to function properly, it also requires sugar but only in moderate amounts. High concentrations burden your pancreas, liver, and adrenals. Not only does it affect your body, but it can affect your emotions as well. Manic-depressive swings may result from sugar addiction. So just like the other addictors, limit your sugar intake.

Life experiences provide everyone with enough stress as it is. Don't add to it with addictions; instead, practice moderation and focus on your priorities for success.

PRACTICAL ACTION STEPS

1. As most of the four addictors are social ones and are often associated with peer pressure, to remain moderate, say "Thanks, but no thanks," to excesses.

2. When you're out, select places where these addictors aren't used excessively. For example, if you go to a bar, you'd probably be persuaded to have a cigarette and a drink. Likewise, you'd probably be tempted to order a coffee and some sugary foods if you go to

a doughnut or sweet shop. To curb your excesses, prioritize where you hang out.

3. If you keep a stock of the four addictors around your house, you'll probably be more tempted to partake because they're too accessible. Don't make it so easy to get to them! Consider unloading your stockpile.

4. Try this experiment for one week: moderate the four addictors (or other ones that you use), and see what differences it makes in your body and general outlook.

After a few days of adjustment involving physical reactions from withdrawal (for instance, possibly suffering from headaches), you'll note soon thereafter that you have more steady energy, clearer focus, and more confidence—all of which will build your success. Once you've finished this weeklong experiment, you probably won't want to return to excesses again.

AFFIRMATION

*I am a master of myself, and my
middle name is moderation.*

Now write your own affirmation in your journal
or on a separate piece of paper.

Secret #16

CONTRACT AND THEN RELAX ALL MUSCLES

Whether or not we're aware of it, we accumulate lots of tension in our bodies throughout each day. From the first jump when the alarm goes off to the frustration of seeking a lost sock, locating misplaced car keys, or dealing with whatever else goes on in the morning, all of these "tensions" accumulate and tense up muscles, usually without us even noticing.

It's so easy to neglect these little irritants, but if you do, they build up one on top of another—like layers of dust or soot—eventually becoming one big ball of tension. To avoid this, I've found the following quick exercise to be a wonderful stress releaser: while either sitting, standing, or lying down, contract *all* of your muscles as if tensing every cell and molecule in your body. After holding yourself completely taut for at least 20 seconds, suddenly let go and feel how all of your tension has just been flushed out.

There are no limitations on the frequency of doing this stress releaser. You may do it during any private moments available to you throughout the day. It can be done so speedily and quickly that you can practice it almost anywhere.

Naturally, if you're in the middle of a conversation with someone—unless that discussion is over the phone and the person on the other end is in the middle of a long monologue—you probably won't want to do this around other people. If you do so, they may become alarmed at the grimace on your face! However, you should have plenty of opportunities—remember to add this stress releaser to your daily routine.

Why not start at this very moment? Try the following muscle-contracting exercise, and see the stress-relieving results for yourself:

- Exhale fully.

- Contract every muscle that you're capable of contracting.

- Tighten, tighten, and tighten some more—and hold!

- Keep holding and tightening for at least 20 seconds.

- Relax, let go, and savor the fabulous release.

If you followed the steps, you now feel a lot more relaxed! It's important that when you do your contractions, contract yourself as tight, tight, tight as possible. When you eventually *let it all go,* you really have something to let go of!

PRACTICAL ACTION STEPS

1. Do this stress releaser at least twice daily, preferably not on a full stomach.

2. Write yourself a note and place it where you can see it as a reminder to do your stress-busting contractions.

AFFIRMATION

I let go of stress by contracting all of my muscles and then relaxing them.

Now write your own affirmation in your journal or on a separate piece of paper.

৵ৎ৵ ৵ৎ৵ ৵ৎ৵

Secret #17

HELP OTHERS FULFILL THEIR GOALS

Whether we imagine ourselves to be anti-social or great socializers who love people, a lone ranger or a party person, we are all part of a master team. The connecting thread weaving through the course of all of our lives joins us in a special way that is indefinable.

We feel greater self-worth and more successful when we provide services for others. There's a touch of the Good Samaritan in all of us; therefore, there is wisdom in setting aside special time in our daily routines for doing something that helps another person.

Let this particular service you engage in be the type that assists others in fulfilling their goals. Sometimes it won't be an immediate "gratifier," but it will take the form of a long-term gain. This follows the ancient proverb: "If you give a man a fish, you feed him for a day. But teach him how to fish, and you will feed him for a lifetime."

This Good Samaritan aspect of ourselves can express itself without us even being aware of it. For example, some of us already live this out by being courteous and opening doors for others or simply helping someone run an errand.

This compassionate trait can also be expressed by playing with children in a park or assisting an elderly person cross the street. Some of us may work or volunteer with a charitable cause. Whatever form this service takes, it should be done in love.

As I stated, one of the greatest gifts we can offer is education—that is, teaching others how to fish for life instead of just handing them a fish. Sometimes, what we perceive as a service to others may ultimately be a means of robbing them of their dignity. However, what I recommend isn't so much about bailing people out, but providing them with opportunities and learning situations that foster self-worth and self-sufficiency.

PRACTICAL ACTION STEPS

The main purpose of helping someone isn't meant to add new stress or burden to your life. Offering help or assistance to others enables *you* to achieve a greater sense of inner success.

1. Each day find a way that you can assist someone else in fulfilling his or her goals whether they're small or large.

2. When you come upon opportunities to be of service, act on them.

3. Think of some of your friends and imagine how you might help them obtain what they would love to have or do in life. If you don't know, simply call and ask them.

AFFIRMATION

*Today, I open my heart, keep my eyes open,
and do what I can to help others.*

Now write your own affirmation in your journal
or on a separate piece of paper.

෴ ෴ ෴

Secret #18

SAVE 5 TO 10 PERCENT OF
YOUR EARNINGS

Imagine that you're teaching a dog to fetch a stick, sit up and beg, or engage in some other act that demands disciplined focus. How do you get the pup to pay attention? You may have your own answer to this situation, but generally, what works best is to offer a reward. In this case, a tasty treat or a pat on the head at the successful execution of the trick works well. Likewise, a great incentive for anyone to complete a task is a reward or recognition for a job well done.

It may seem like a poor analogy to equate a person's motivation to that of a dog learning a new trick, but unless we encourage and reward the different facets of *ourselves*—which must endure change in order to

accomplish goals and move us from stress to success—
our inner selves are likely to mutiny, causing our focus
and determination to fall away. We also need something
to spur us on to continued greater endeavors.

One way in which you can really experience this is
by putting money in a savings account and watching
it grow over time. Figure out how much you earn a
day, and then deposit 5 to 10 percent of it into your
account. I call this the "Behavior Reward Account." I
make regular deposits in my own BRA—not IRA.

You naturally don't need to deposit your savings
daily. You can work out your weekly or monthly 5 to
10 percent reward rate. But I've found that the more
frequently you add to your savings, the more you'll save
and feel rewarded. The longer the time span you leave
between making actual deposits, then the more likely
it is that the money you've put aside will be swallowed
up by other priorities.

Saving money not only helps you feel more abundant
and successful, but it's also a great incentive. As savings
grow, so, too, does your motivation. In addition, it's
inspirational and helpful if whatever you're saving

isn't simply used for an immediate gratification or even designated for "rainy days." It's much wiser to have a bigger picture of what your BRA savings are going to achieve.

I've realized that when we save for a purpose that's larger than ourselves—possibly even for something lasting longer than our own lifetimes—this can be our most successful savings incentive. In fact, it's easier to save for a bigger, long-term cause than a less significant, short-term one. Therefore, when organizing savings, we should think in terms of how it will impact the future.

For example, imagine that one of your friends asked you for a loan in order to pay overdue bills. You'd probably say no and feel rather uncomfortable and upset by the request. But if your friend asked you to provide money for something in which you believed was bigger than the both of you (such as establishing a foundation for a worthy cause), your reaction to parting with your money would be a lot different.

One last way of rewarding yourself, reducing stress, and building success involves the importance of paying yourself *first*. People who pay themselves first put a greater value on themselves; they get ahead and experience more success. But those who pay themselves last devalue themselves and fall behind.

PRACTICAL ACTION STEPS

1. Open your own BRA (Behavior Reward Account) today!

2. Deposit 5 to 10 percent of whatever your income is into this account daily, weekly, or monthly—the more frequently, the better!

3. Determine the ultimate purpose for your savings.

4. Keep focused on this long-term goal.

5. Make sure you don't let anything else interfere with this objective.

AFFIRMATIONS

*Through my savings, I am growing richer and more
abundant day by day. I pay myself first.*

Now write your own affirmation in your journal
or on a separate piece of paper.

→← →← →←

Secret #19

WRITE THREE THANK-YOU LETTERS

Have you ever received a sincere thank-you letter in the mail and felt how it transformed your day? What a heart-opening experience it can be to receive such a thoughtful note! Thank-yous are not only rewarding for the recipient, but they are equally satisfying and inspiring for the sender.

The power of thank-you letters isn't limited to the actual sending and receiving; they have a special energy just in their idea. In fact, a grateful thought put to paper without even being sent is still tremendously rewarding.

Writing thank-you letters can be one of the easiest exercises of all in order to change stress into success.

Toward the end of each day, spend a moment reflecting on earlier events. Consider which people throughout the day actually served you the most. They don't have to be individuals who actually did something helpful for you.

Sometimes, the people who stand in the way and create obstacles are actually helping the most because they confront you and force you to come up with your best, enabling you to become a greater achiever.

Therefore, don't limit your thank-you letters to those who've made your life easier in some fashion. Be sure to show gratitude to the people who've made it harder for you—in their way, they've helped you develop true grit.

To those who've challenged you or offered support, you can write long thank-you letters, short ones, or just tiny little notes. You can send them or save them or do whatever you want with them.

An important ingredient in opening your heart and seeing life as it truly is—a blessed and magnificent series of events—is to consider your day. Reflect upon your blessings and put your thank-yous on paper.

PRACTICAL ACTION STEPS

1. Set a time aside (possibly before going to bed) to consider what has occurred throughout the day. As you look back through the day's events, consider which three individuals have served you well and made your life richer or more enlightened in some fashion.

2. Write these individuals a thank-you letter from your heart, expressing your acknowledgment of the role they've played in your life and how their presence is of wonderful service to you.

AFFIRMATIONS

I reflect upon my day, and I am grateful.
I write my three thank-you letters daily.

Now write your own affirmation in your journal or on a separate piece of paper.

෴ ෴ ෴

Secret #20

REWARD YOURSELF FOR YOUR ACCOMPLISHMENTS

As I stated in Secret #18, rewarding yourself for your achievements and continued success is important. Saving money is one way to do so, but there are many other methods. Often, no one is going to reward you for a job well done, so if you don't take the time to recognize your own hard work and efforts, you won't truly experience and appreciate how much you've accomplished. Success in life demands self-acknowledgment.

As an example, I'd like to share a true story from my late wife, Athena:

While windsurfing at Palm Beach in Australia, I managed to complete a very tricky three-point turn against heavy gale-force winds. High on my accomplishment, I raced back to land to see if everybody sitting on the shore had witnessed it, but to my dismay, they'd all been looking the other way. I was incredibly deflated and letdown. Fortunately, Midget Farrelly, a former world-champion surfer, took me aside and said, "Athena, when you achieve your greatest successes, usually, no one will see it or be there to reward you. Therefore, get into the habit of always acknowledging and rewarding yourself."

Creating the discipline of self-acknowledgment for your successes is important. Nobody will build you up as much as you can . . . or, for that matter, put you down as much as you can. One builds success, and the other leads to stress. You are your own best praiser *and* worst critic.

Oftentimes, we've developed the habit of being tough on ourselves, and too seldom do we reward ourselves for what we've achieved. Instead of looking at ourselves with criticism, we must replace the judgment with acknowledgment.

Go out of your way to acknowledge your triumphs! Recognize your everyday heroic abilities to conquer your own inner and outer dragons. Give yourself some type of reward for doing so well in life and for doing your best on all occasions. This can transform stress to success!

PRACTICAL ACTION STEPS

1. First decide on the types of rewards you'd love to receive. Maybe this could take the form of a night out to dinner, a gift to yourself, a massage or facial, or simply some special time for relaxation.

2. Reward yourself with whatever method seems appropriate for your various accomplishments. The key in the reward is the feeling of acknowledgment for success.

AFFIRMATION

I acknowledge myself for succeeding
and reward myself with love.

Now write your own affirmation in your journal
or on a separate piece of paper.

ഇംഗ ഇംഗ ഇംഗ

Secret #21

EXPRESS FEELINGS OF LOVE

Expressing your sincere feelings of love could be considered the epitome of success, for true success demands the expression of your heartfelt love. When your heart is open and filled with gratitude and love, you attract the people, places, things, ideas, or events that will help you build the life you've dreamed of. Conversely, when your heart is closed and blocked off to love, you end up attracting more stressful calamities.

Therefore, it's important to set aside time at the beginning and end of each day to feel and think about what you love in your life. By focusing on these people or things, your heart automatically opens. The way in which you open your heart and feel love will differ from others. For example, you may feel or think about several things, but someone else may focus on a specific person, child, or pet. And still others may think about a wonderful meal they had enjoyed or a scene from the natural world, such as a sunrise or sunset. You may even think about a funny situation that occurred in the day!

It doesn't matter what you use to open the door to your heart. What does matter is that you start and finish your day with the expression of love-filled energy and thoughts.

Throughout each day, there are many subtle or more obvious ways you can express your feelings of love to others. In the office or at your workplace, just telling someone how great he or she looks can really put a golden glow into the air. And when others have performed a service for you, take the time to tell them what a magnificent job they've done.

Expressing love can take many forms. Naturally, you are wise to tell those you really care about—be it your beloved, your children, or your parents—how much you love them. The words *I love you* can really open hearts and clear the air. There's no greater way to build success than through love!

PRACTICAL ACTION STEPS

1. Sit quietly and think about the people, places, things, ideas, and events in your life that you love. Visualize these situations or people as if they were around you right now. Be thankful for their presence in your life and the gift that loving them has given you. Feel your heart open wide, and be grateful for the love that surrounds you.

2. Now think of a practical way in which you can actually express these feelings in your daily life, such as a gift of flowers, a hug, a phone call, a simple "I love you," or whatever else will reflect the love inside you.

AFFIRMATION

I express my feelings of love daily, and what I express outwardly is returned to my heart.

Now write your own affirmation in your journal or on a separate piece of paper.

Secret #22

HUG SOMEONE SPECIAL

One of the greatest feelings in life is when those you love wrap their arms around you. Wow—don't hugs feel fabulous? Of course, you don't have to limit them to family members or to those who are dear to you.

We can hug our co-workers, friends, teammates, and many others we encounter every day. In fact, most of us give and receive too few hugs and could benefit from giving and receiving more!

Now I'm not recommending that you just walk up to somebody indiscriminately and hug him or her (although in special cases, this may work out nicely)— that would be an unwise use of hugs. But I do suggest that you take the time to hug daily. However, this can require careful attention because some of us aren't as adept at closeness as others.

There can be valuable reasons for keeping some people at arm's length, but many of us have taken this too far. Frequently, we put up unnecessary barriers to those we could easily hug, such as our parents, siblings, close friends, relatives, and co-workers.

So, when opportunities arise to express love and gratitude, take advantage of them and don't let these moments slip by. There are times throughout any day when a hug can say more than a thousand words. When this occurs, shine your light (in the form of a hug) on this situation!

A hug is a heart-to-heart expression. If you can't find a person to embrace, hugging a pet, tree, or just about anything else (even a pillow) can be a move in this wise direction. The value of a hug is enormous. It reduces stress and provides you with an inner calmness that leads to success.

PRACTICAL ACTION STEPS

The secret to remember is that sincere and appropriate hugs help transform stress into success.

1. Keep your eyes open for "hug opportunities" throughout the day and night.

2. When an appropriate time arises, put your arms out and seize the moment with a giant hug.

3. See how many hugs you can give or receive in one day. The rewards will show for themselves!

AFFIRMATION

I am a shining hugger, and I embrace everything with love!

Now write your own affirmation in your journal or on a separate piece of paper.

෨෨෨ ෨෨෨ ෨෨෨

Secret #23

CLEAN AND ORGANIZE
YOUR ENVIRONMENT

Have you ever noticed that a cluttered outer environment can leave you with a cluttered inner feeling? Well, I certainly have! Whenever your surroundings are messy and disorganized—particularly at the start of a day—you may have noticed that by the end of the day, things become even more untidy, and you feel increasingly chaotic. Clutter leads to scatter, and scatter leads to stress.

We waste so much valuable time and energy looking for things or sorting through piles of paper and useless paraphernalia when our environments are cluttered. Disorganization also keeps us from staying focused on top-priority actions.

Sometimes we spend twice as much energy just looking for something that might be right under our noses because we never took the time to put it in its own special place.

So, before commencing your day, organize your work space or environment so that you have as little clutter or mess as possible. Empty garbage bins, throw out dead flowers, tidy up, and make the things around you not only more accessible but also more attractive.

Clutter creates confusion, and organization creates flow and harmony. Some people, however, claim that they work best in clutter, but they probably just haven't discovered what powerhouses they could be if they kept their spaces organized.

In a systematized work space, those who claim that clutter works best for them are likely to find themselves to be twice, three times, or even a hundred times more productive than they are now . . . if they ever have an opportunity to experience this over any period of time.

PRACTICAL ACTION STEPS

1. Before beginning any activity, sort out your environment. If you have a desk or work space, start there first. Clean it up and organize. Put everything in its place.

2. Tackle organizing your environment one step at a time: one space, one room, and one closet or drawer at a time. Don't overwhelm yourself and end up creating new stress.

3. At the end of your day, put things back where they belong so that you'll start the next day with a tidy and organized environment.

AFFIRMATION

I organize my environment and feel successful in my life.

Now write your own affirmation in your journal or on a separate piece of paper.

Secret #24

ELIMINATE LOW-PRIORITY "UNNECESSITIES"

Most of us are creatures of habit—often stress-producing habits. We all have our routines that we've carried out for years, and we seldom alter our behavior unless we first consciously think about it. Some of these routines consume considerable time and energy, making them investments in low-priority "unnecessities."

Often, stressful habits involve chores or actions that you don't even like to do in the first place. In fact, your routine can be filled to the brim with things that decrease your productivity, success, and well-being. Therefore, take a thorough look at how you spend your time. Determine which activities truly serve you and which ones don't.

Examples of low-priority unnecessities may include: taking a coffee or cigarette break every hour just because it's the hour; opening and scanning your mail, putting it down to completely read it later, and then reading junk mail or other unimportant materials; going to the supermarket without first compiling a shopping list and then needing to return later; or even dropping dirty or just-worn clothes on the floor that just have to be picked up later.

There are so many little things in each day that create busyness and waste—and *not* success. Such unnecessities rob us of valuable time, which could be used for higher priority actions. It's amazing how easily we can become stuck in habits that lead to stress. Eliminate your low-priority unnecessities!

This stress-to-success secret wouldn't be complete without also mentioning another unnecessary action: wasted time on telephones. Think of all the time you've spent listening to someone go on and on about something that you aren't remotely interested in simply because you didn't speak up and say that you have other things to do. Don't allow other people's trivial matters—or your own—take up your valuable time.

PRACTICAL ACTION STEPS

1. Stop reading this book right now and write down all of the low-priority, unnecessary actions that you do throughout any day.

2. Review this list and then jot down specific higher priority actions that will take their place. In some cases, no action is needed. (Many low-priority items can be completely eliminated without being replaced.)

3. Keep this list with you and review it as often as needed until your old habits have been transformed into the new ones. If you don't focus on high-priority activities, you'll continue wasting time and increasing your stress.

AFFIRMATIONS

I serve myself through all of my high-priority actions, thoughts, and deeds. I eliminate "unnecessities."

Now write your own affirmation in your journal or on a separate piece of paper.

Secret #25

STUDY THE SUBJECT YOU'D LOVE TO MASTER

Many of us would like to learn another language or master some subject in life. Instead of wishing that we had a particular area of knowledge or talent, it's much wiser to just set aside the necessary space and time to obtain it. *Everyone* has enough time.

As little as five or ten minutes a day can be all that it takes to achieve your desires. If you focus yourself and seriously study a specific language or subject, you can eventually master it.

Since life is a journey made up of many steps, learning new skills demands that you start somewhere and "some*when*" on that path. The sooner you begin gathering information, the sooner you'll gain an understanding and mastery. Why wait?

Procrastination adds stress, but action leads to success. Therefore, go out and buy some books or learning tapes on whatever subject you'd love to know more about. You could also simply go to the library and start researching. Invest at least ten minutes a day in study. Instead of this subject being a mystery, you can make it your mastery.

It's been said that if one studies a specific topic or field for just 30 minutes each day, he or she can be a leader in that particular subject within seven to ten years. Because this appears so, there's no limit on what you can do with your success. Any topic you love is yours to devour and master.

Successful people aren't always the ones who've been formally educated; oftentimes, they're self-taught. So if you would love to master a new language or topic, just do it! It may take you to the top of your field.

PRACTICAL ACTION STEPS

1. Think about a subject or skill you'd love to master, and then go out and find which references, books, DVDs, or CDs will serve you best in achieving your goal.

2. Set aside at least five to ten minutes every day, investing your time exclusively on that subject. If you feel you can set aside 30 minutes, know that you'll be able to reach the top of that field even sooner.

3. Celebrate while you learn. All types of knowledge, however small, can add to your success. Don't give up! Perseverance pays off. Every little piece of information you glean adds to the big picture.

4. Integrate and organize everything you learn. Organized knowledge will create a masterpiece, but disorganized knowledge will create stress.

AFFIRMATIONS

*I study what I would love to master. I am learning in
leaps and bounds every day in every way!*

Now write your own affirmation in your journal
or on a separate piece of paper.

⌒⌒   ⌒⌒   ⌒⌒

Secret #26

SPEND TIME IN TOTAL MEDITATIVE SILENCE

There is a constant flow of inspiring messages coming to us from unknown higher sources. If we wish to receive these messages of love, guidance, and poise, all that's required of us is to spend a few moments in total meditative silence.

When our days are stressful and chaotic—overrun by deadlines and hustle and bustle—we often become so preoccupied that we forget to take time to open up to receiving this success-filled, inspiring guidance. I like to call the source of these messages our "Cosmic Mailbox in the Sky."

Designating a part of each day (even if it's just for a few moments) for solitude and inner reflection is time well spent. Meditative silence can fire you up like no other activity or form of exercise!

In fact, Einstein claimed that he gained insights to the profound questions in his life by allowing his mind to travel on a light beam to these higher sources. The messages he received were the answers that he'd been seeking. Today, the guidance he attained (and then expressed to the world) has become immortal.

Allow yourself to explore this same method of inspired guidance just like Einstein. Sit quietly and let your heart and mind be open to receiving information from your higher source, or soul (or whatever else you may personally like to call these higher realms of inspiration).

Relax into the quietness within yourself where you feel as if you rise out of your own body, or where you quiet down so much within yourself that external thoughts or activities are no longer relevant. In this state of inner peacefulness, your higher sources will be able to speak to you. Be patient. If you're open, they will speak and guide you wisely. Through this wisdom, you'll gain greater success.

PRACTICAL ACTION STEPS

1. Find a place where you can sit quietly and remain uninterrupted for a few minutes each day.

2. Set aside any stressful thoughts that may prevent you from relaxing. Let yourself go until you obtain a deep, totally silent meditative state.

3. Let the ever-present and inspiring messages fill your mind as you ask for their higher guidance. Leave yourself open and receptive to whatever wisdom comes to you from this higher source.

4. Keep a piece of paper and pencil close by so you can record any messages as you receive them. Some of the greatest stress-dissolving and success-building ideas can be received this way.

5. If you're having difficulty relaxing and letting go, think about everything you're grateful for in life. This will help you attain deep and inspiring meditative silence.

AFFIRMATIONS

I am silent, and my heart is open.
I meditate to receive inspiring, guiding messages daily.

Now write your own affirmation in your journal or on a separate piece of paper.

～ ～ ～

Secret #27

MASSAGE YOUR BODY OR SCALP

Many of us love to receive massages, but some people don't like to be touched by others at all. We are all individuals and, therefore, have our own personal preferences, but for the purposes of transforming stress into success in just 31 days, this practice can be very helpful. A professional massage once a week can be immensely beneficial, particularly if you and your massage therapist are "in tune."

If having a weekly professional massage isn't realistic, try to make time each day—preferably in the evening before retiring—to massage yourself. This can work wonders on your mind and body.

I've found that briskly massaging the scalp releases an enormous amount of stress. It can also alleviate a tension headache. If you have a partner who's loving and willing to do this for you, it can be even more relaxing because then you can totally get into the feeling of letting your stress clear out of your head.

It can be equally relaxing to massage other parts of your body, too, including your feet, hands, Achilles tendon, and face. Everybody has their own particular areas where they accumulate tension.

As you massage yourself (or as someone massages you), just focus on any areas that are extra tense. If your hands can't endure long sessions of self-massage, there are several excellent electric handheld massage tools that can act as substitutes.

PRACTICAL ACTION STEPS

1. Determine which areas of your body are the most tense.

2. Before retiring for the evening, spend several minutes massaging your scalp and the other tense areas of your body (you may also ask your partner to massage you).

3. Don't stop until all of your tension and stress are gone. This can contribute to a deep and restful night's sleep.

AFFIRMATION

I help my body center itself by lovingly energizing it through massage.

Now write your own affirmation in your journal or on a separate piece of paper.

Secret #28

TAKE A HOT BATH BEFORE RETIRING

Water is an incredibly powerful element of nature. A baby in the womb swims in its earliest bath within the amniotic sac. Our bodies comprise an awesome quantity of water (some 90 percent). Even the profound spiritual ritual known as baptism is often done by totally submerging recipients in water.

There's something mystical about water. It helps us make transformations that alter our entire physical, mental, and spiritual outlook.

Just think about how a bath refreshes and relaxes you!

The regenerative and healing qualities of a hot bath can't be questioned. How often have you felt exhausted or stressed but noticed that after a hot bath, you feel totally new and energized? Tense muscles and aches and pains seem to just melt during a submersion in a long, warm, and relaxing bath.

I recommend taking a hot bath each night because this is an ideal time to relax. Generally, showers perk you up, whereas a good soak tends to ease and relax the body. While you're enjoying a relaxing bath, consider including candlelight, soft music, soothing bath oils, or whatever else it takes to make the moment magical for you.

Some people—usually guys—hate baths with a vengeance. For those who truly dislike reclining in the tub, you can simply fill a basin with hot water and sponge yourself down to achieve similar results. This can be a very meditative and relaxing alternative.

In addition, when you go to sleep after a relaxing bath, you'll often receive insights during the night that help you solve the next day's challenges. Baths return you to the peaceful state of the womb and prepare you for tomorrow's success!

PRACTICAL ACTION STEPS

1. As part of your bedtime routine, be sure to either take a hot bath or sponge yourself down.

2. Create a calming and peaceful atmosphere. Turn off ringing phones, blaring TVs, and other distractions.

3. Play soft, gentle music (maybe classical music, if you wish). This can greatly enhance your relaxation process.

4. This is a terrific time to visualize tomorrow's priorities for success.

AFFIRMATION

I use nature's power in the form of water to wash away my stress and plan for my success.

Now write your own affirmation in your journal or on a separate piece of paper.

∽∂ ∽∂ ∽∂

Secret #29

COUNT YOUR BLESSINGS
WITH GRATITUDE

Gratitude is the creator of miracles. Grateful thoughts empower you and make you feel lighter, as they open up your heart and allow you to feel the love that is always inwardly present. Feeling thankful eases the tensions of daily life. Gratefulness heals, soothes, and enlightens.

Gratitude turns a day of stress into a day of fulfillment. It's the secret of success! Success is born from gratitude, and stress is born from ingratitude. Stop for a moment and reflect on the many magnificent events and people that you've had the opportunity to experience today.

A heart that has been opened by gratitude can transform any crisis into a blessing and opportunity. Truly successful people are grateful people.

Count your blessings each night, and end your day with thanks. Faster than any other state of mind, gratitude can transform stress into success. It provides a mental rocket-ship ride to the next inspiring experience in your life.

So if you want to hold a "ticket" within yourself—in your awareness—that will transport you onward and upward toward greater success and away from stress, then be appreciative. See that all of the circumstances surrounding your life, no matter what they are, are just lessons in gratitude.

PRACTICAL ACTION STEPS

1. Close your eyes and think about a time when a difficult situation became a blessing —where you had to move into the future to see a challenge as an opportunity. Now review any difficulties that have occurred today, and project the possible benefits that

they will offer in the future. They're sure to provide some blessings. This is the art of being grateful.

2. Write down these blessings and focus on them.

3. Maintain a gratitude attitude, regardless of how life seems to challenge you. There are no crises without equal and opposite blessings. Wisdom is the instantaneous recognition of this fact.

4. See how fast you can recognize the hidden blessings behind current crises. This act alone will transform your stress into success and is one of the wisest action steps you can do each day.

AFFIRMATIONS

I am thankful for my gifts today.
My heart is filled with gratitude!

Now write your own affirmation in your journal or on a separate piece of paper.

Secret #30

GET A GOOD NIGHT'S REST

There's something joyously liberating about waking up early and springing out of bed with enthusiasm and fire, ready to accomplish all of your goals without stress.

It's wise to set out on the day's journey early. But to get up early demands that you retire at a reasonable hour. Successful people spring out of bed, but stressed people just crawl out reluctantly.

Those who stay up late tend to sleep in late. Over-sleeping can steal our lives away, just as not getting enough sleep can. A lot of us spend many hours sleeping not because we want to, but because we're attempting to release the stress or anxieties that were accumulated during the days before. Another reason could be that we're nervous and worrying about what the future holds.

When you aren't doing what you love and loving what you do, you're more likely to sleep too much because when you're awake, you're doing things you don't love!

In some cases, when you aren't doing what you enjoy, anxiety and depression can keep you from sleeping, and this is just as debilitating as too much sleep. Without enough sleep, you may feel groggy and grumpy. In addition, your metabolic rate slows down.

All of these negative symptoms can be extremely stressful in itself and rob you of the fire you require for your day of success!

It's much more beneficial to go to bed early and wake up early. In fact, there's great wisdom in the expression "The early bird gets the worm." If you get a good night's rest and wake up early, your day is off to a great start.

However, it's hard to accomplish this if you consume excessive food or drink right before bed. As I stated earlier, this can make you feel sluggish on awakening and throughout the next day. Therefore, some discipline is required.

PRACTICAL ACTION STEPS

1. Eat early so that your food has time to digest before you retire.

2. Pick an hour to wake up in the morning that allows you extra time to do some thankfulness exercises, stretching, and generally prepare yourself to make the most of the new day.

3. Get to bed at a reasonable hour.

4. Wake up at the exact time you set, and spring out of bed focused on your success. (You'll have the energy to do so after a healthy, restful night of sleep!)

AFFIRMATIONS

*I am an early bird! I go to bed early
and greet the new day with joy.*

Now write your own affirmation in your journal
or on a separate piece of paper.

༄ ༄ ༄

Secret #31

FOLLOW A STRESS-TO-SUCCESS CHECKLIST

Have you ever come across a great idea or system and decided that you'd act on it, but then forgot to do so because you didn't write it down and couldn't remember exactly what you needed to do? Have you found it difficult to stay inspired and focused on your success as you confront everyday stresses? Well, I've experienced this in the past and found that it's helpful to create a daily list that I read and check off each morning and evening to serve as a reminder and guide throughout the day.

Following a checklist is wise. Anything that we can put down on paper and not leave running around in our heads helps us reduce stress and adds to our successes. They say that a short pencil is better than a long memory! Habits can make us or break us. Maintaining a routine of high-priority action steps will put us on the road to success.

Although there are 31 success secrets in this book, you may certainly add more as you discover your own success secrets over time. There's something magical and incredibly fulfilling about checking off your accomplishments. A daily checklist can help you stay on task and transform your stress into success.

PRACTICAL ACTION STEPS

These action steps complement the Daily Stress-to-Success Checklist, which is the following section in this book. Make copies of the checklist, and use them over the next 31 days to help you reduce stress and build success. As you do so, keep these steps in mind:

1. Review the Stress-to-Success Checklist every morning. Make it a priority to do as many—if not all—of the 31 secrets as possible each day.

2. In the evening, review your checklist and rate yourself according to the instructions.

3. On the following morning, focus on accomplishing the secrets that you may not have done to the fullest the previous day.

4. Use this checklist as your guide for the next 31 days. Welcome to a more success-filled life!

AFFIRMATION

I follow my success checklist daily,
for I know the value of a checkup from the neck up!

Now write your own affirmation in your journal or on a separate piece of paper.

Daily Stress-to-Success Checklist

Watch yourself transform stress into the motivation and inspiration needed to live a more fulfilling life. If you incorporate the 31 success secrets into your daily routine, you'll be empowered to achieve your goals and realize your dreams.

For the next 31 days, as you review the checklist in the evening, evaluate yourself in order to track your progress toward success. Rate yourself according to the following numbers, and then simply total up your score.

1 = Not at all
2 = A little
3 = Moderately
4 = A lot
5 = Totally

Today, did you . . .

☐ 1. Write and read your goals.
☐ 2. Clear away your goal's obstacles.
☐ 3. Prioritize your activities.
☐ 4. Act on top priorities.
☐ 5. Visualize your success.
☐ 6. Write and read your affirmations.
☐ 7. Practice deep breathing and stretching.
☐ 8. Do selective and collective reading.
☐ 9. Groom for success.

- [ ] 10. Dress for success.
- [ ] 11. Love what you do and do what you love.
- [ ] 12. Surround yourself with succeeders.
- [ ] 13. Drink lots of water.
- [ ] 14. Eat light, moderate meals.
- [ ] 15. Reduce the four "addictors."
- [ ] 16. Contract and then relax all muscles.
- [ ] 17. Help others fulfill their goals.
- [ ] 18. Save 5 to 10 percent of your earnings.
- [ ] 19. Write three thank-you letters.
- [ ] 20. Reward yourself for your accomplishments.
- [ ] 21. Express feelings of love.
- [ ] 22. Hug someone special.
- [ ] 23. Clean and organize your environment.
- [ ] 24. Eliminate low-priority "unnecessities."
- [ ] 25. Study the subject you'd love to master.
- [ ] 26. Spend time in total meditative silence.
- [ ] 27. Massage your body or scalp.
- [ ] 28. Take a hot bath before retiring.
- [ ] 29. Count your blessings with gratitude.
- [ ] 30. Get a good night's rest.
- [ ] 31. Follow a Stress-to-Success Checklist.

31–60 = High Stress
61–90 = Moderate Stress
91–120 = Moderate Success
121–155 = High Success

◄◙► ◄◙► ◄◙►

About the Author

Dr. John F. Demartini is an international speaker and consultant who breathes life and enthusiasm into his audiences with his enlightening perspectives, humorous observations of human nature, and practical action steps. When he speaks, hearts open, minds become inspired, and people are motivated into action. His gentle, fun, and informative teachings mingle entertaining stories with transformational wisdom and insights. His trailblazing philosophy and revolutionary understanding are reshaping modern psychology and business and transforming the lives of millions. As a retired chiropractor, researcher, writer, and philosopher, his studies have made him a leading expert on healing, human potential, and philosophy.

Dr. Demartini is the founder of the Demartini Institute, which includes the Studies of Wisdom research and the Concourse of Wisdom educational divisions.

He is also the creator of The Breakthrough Experience®
seminar and originator of The Demartini Method™ and
The Great Discovery™. He has written several dozens
of books, including the bestsellers *Count Your Blessings:
The Healing Power of Gratitude and Love; The Breakthrough
Experience: A Revolutionary New Approach to Personal
Transformation; How to Make One Hell of a Profit and Still
Get to Heaven; You Can Have an Amazing Life . . . in Just
60 Days!; The Heart of Love: How to Go Beyond Fantasy to
Find True Relationship Fulfillment;* and *The Riches Within:
Your Seven Secret Treasures.*

Articles and feature stories about Dr. Demartini and
his insightful personal and professional development
methodologies have appeared in numerous international
magazines and newspapers. He's appeared on hundreds
of radio and television news and talk shows and several
film documentaries. As a presenter, Dr. Demartini has
shared his transformative principles and methodologies
in conferences with business executives, health
professionals, financial managers, and consultants
working in the field of human consciousness; and
he has presented alongside many of the most well-
respected speaking professionals today. As a pioneer on
the frontier of human consciousness and an explorer
of the ultimate nature of reality, Dr. Demartini is also a

leader in the field of psycho-spiritual development and transformation.

In addition, Dr. Demartini is a private consultant, advising people from all walks of life on personal and professional development and achievement. These include Wall Street financiers, corporate executives, health professionals, politicians, Hollywood stars, and sports personalities. His many clients use his expertise and wisdom to assist in keeping their lives, health, relationships, attitudes, and business acumen steadily on track.

For more information:
(888) DEMARTINI or (713) 850-1234
Fax: 713-850-9239
www.DrDemartini.com

Notes

Notes

Hay House Titles of Related Interest

YOU CAN HEAL YOUR LIFE, the movie,
starring Louise L. Hay & Friends
(available as a 1-DVD program and
an expanded 2-DVD set)
Watch the trailer at: **www.LouiseHayMovie.com**

THE SHIFT, the movie,
starring Dr. Wayne W. Dyer
(available as a 1-DVD program and
an expanded 2-DVD set)
Watch the trailer at: **www.DyerMovie.com**

AN ATTITUDE OF GRATITUDE: *21 Life Lessons,*
by Keith D. Harrell

CREATIVE FLOWDREAMING™: *Manifesting Your Dreams
in the Life You've Already Got,* by Summer McStravick

EXCUSES BEGONE! *How to Change Lifelong, Self-Defeating
Thinking Habits,* by Dr. Wayne W. Dyer

HEALTH BLISS: *50 Revitalizing NatureFoods & Lifestyle
Choices to Promote Vibrant Health,*
by Susan Smith Jones, Ph.D.

MONEY, AND THE LAW OF ATTRACTION:
Learning to Attract Wealth, Health, and Happiness, by Esther
and Jerry Hicks (The Teachings of Abraham®)

SECRETS OF SUCCESS: *The Science and Spirit of Real Prosperity,* by Sandra Anne Taylor and Sharon A. Klinger

10 SECRETS FOR SUCCESS AND INNER PEACE, by Dr. Wayne W. Dyer

All of the above are available at your local bookstore, or may be ordered by contacting Hay House (see last page).

We hope you enjoyed this Hay House book. If you'd like to receive our online catalog featuring additional information on Hay House books and products, or if you'd like to find out more about the Hay Foundation, please contact:

Hay House, Inc.
P.O. Box 5100
Carlsbad, CA 92018-5100

(760) 431-7695 or **(800) 654-5126**
(760) 431-6948 (fax) or **(800) 650-5115 (fax)**
www.hayhouse.com® • **www.hayfoundation.org**

Published and distributed in Australia by:
Hay House Australia Pty. Ltd., 18/36 Ralph St., Alexandria NSW 2015 •
Phone: 612-9669-4299 • *Fax:* 612-9669-4144 • www.hayhouse.com.au

Published and distributed in the United Kingdom by: Hay House UK, Ltd.,
292B Kensal Rd., London W10 5BE • *Phone:* 44-20-8962-1230 •
Fax: 44-20-8962-1239 • www.hayhouse.co.uk

Published and distributed in the Republic of South Africa by: Hay House SA
(Pty), Ltd., P.O. Box 990, Witkoppen 2068 • *Phone/Fax:* 27-11-467-8904 •
orders@psdprom.co.za • www.hayhouse.co.za

Published in India by: Hay House Publishers India, Muskaan Complex,
Plot No. 3, B-2, Vasant Kunj, New Delhi 110 070 • *Phone:* 91-11-4176-1620 •
Fax: 91-11-4176-1630 • www.hayhouse.co.in

Distributed in Canada by: Raincoast, 9050 Shaughnessy St., Vancouver, B.C.
V6P 6E5 • *Phone:* (604) 323-7100 • *Fax:* (604) 323-2600 •
www.raincoast.com

Take Your Soul on a Vacation

Visit **www.YouCanHealYourLife.com®** to regroup, recharge, and reconnect with your own magnificence. Featuring blogs, mind-body-spirit news, and life-changing wisdom from Louise Hay and friends.

Visit **www.YouCanHealYourLife.com** today!